The Mortal Art: A Collection of Words and Poetry

Sidhaya Pravda Gravador

BookLeaf Publishing

Presentation by *BookLeaf Publishing*

Web: www.bookleafpub.com

E-mail: info@bookleafpub.com

ISBN: 9789357615136

First edition 2022

For all my friends, who always stood by me,

This one's for you.

ACKNOWLEDGEMENT

I express my deep and humbled gratitude to my parents. My number one supporters since the day I was born.

PREFACE

Trigger Warning:
This book contains mentions of suicide and self harm.

The Mortal Art

For the writers, for the poets,
For the sleepless, for the sonnets,
For the ballads and the finches,
For the mortal arts in ditches.

A silent song plays in the distance
A writer stays awake at night
Fingers bleeding like the heart
What a sorry way to make some sorry art

Pouring out your words on a space as white as
snow
Bleeding out your blood and painting it a holy
red
Where words come across or come as they are as
an echo
Of redundancy and melancholic woe

Repeating silent nightmares haunt you every
night
"You're just not good enough" so here you write
Repeating silent nightmares haunt you in the day
"You will never be good enough" so as you write
you pray

The gods will beckon your call I suppose
As long as you keep writing lovely poems and
prose
Don't stop at your tracks, don't stop on your toes
Keep at it and bleed, even if nobody knows

All Our Tales Are Thoughts

For the writers, for the poets;
The singers, songwriters;
For all the wrongdoers.

All our tales, are thoughts.
Mere words that can't be written.
Mere worlds that can't be lived in.

All our tales, are thoughts.
All our tales are thoughts.
Mere breaths our minds cannot exhale.

Strong meth, strong winds, strong hail.
All our tales are thoughts.
All our tales are thoughts.

At last, we breathe, we write.

Pain Over Nothing (The Sorrow)

I'd rather truly cry than wear a fake smile
I'd rather truly lie than tell false truths
I'd rather truly die than just exist
I'm in great pain, please help me
I'd rather have pain over nothing
I'd rather have the rain over sunshine
I'd rather have the slain die not in vain
We're all in great pain, please help us
For having truly cried, i know it's worth
For having truly lied, i know it's purpose
For having truly died, i know it's weight in gold
We are in great pain, and only one can save us

Do Not Submit (Resist)

Do not let yourself be bound by puppet strings,
Do not let yourself be tied up and silenced,
Do not let yourself hang by a thread,
Resist!

Do not let yourself be chained to past mistakes
and sins,
Do not let yourself be troubled by where's and
when's,
Do not let yourself exist but stay dead,
I urge you, resist!

Do not submit to the injustices from ever since,
Do not submit to the dishonesty of the world and
its livid lies and,
Do not be wrought by overgrowth of its
contradictions, like a bullet to the head,
Again and again, resist!

These Days

These days, emptiness is closer than a friend
These days, it seems as if there is no end
These days, it feels like an endless night
For in these days, nothing ever feels right
These days, people come flummoxed and
perplexed
These days, people run with weary feet
These days, it seems no words just can express
The danger of these days, it rests on cushioned
seats
These days, people starve and people hunger
These days, restless nights with nary a slumber
These days, it's like diving into a sea without
any water
These days, it's our hope that's crushed to falter
These days, hollow words are spoken
These days, many promises are broken
These days, nobody's even
In these days, nobody's forgiven
These days, it feels so full of dread
These days, there are some who's fled by even
bread
These days, when this god-forsaken plague
spreads

These days, there are those who hang by a
thread
These days, it grows only ever frightful
These days, nobody seems so rightful
In these days, for praise on which to give
For these days, nay these days do not forgive

In the Instance that I should go to Sleep

In the instance that I should fall to my knees
I'd beg of you to do away with me
I'd close my eyes as I beg and plead
For Life to permit my endless sleep

In the instance that I should fail to wake
Be not alarmed, do not be swayed
We all know it's perhaps for the best
If I should finally be laid to rest

In the instance that I begin to weep
Hear me I plead, for my dry eyes speak
If I should sorrow, I then request
That tomorrow I be laid to rest

However, I Still Love You

However much she dreads me,
I will always love her so
However much she slights me,
There's not a chance that I would go,
And if only I could tell her,
I would let her know.

However much she hates me,
I will forever love her so,
In whatever way she sees me,
She could say what she would although,
If only I could tell her,
I would let her know.

However much she spites me,
At every turn I'd love her so,
However much it hurts me,
My tears I'll never show,
For if only I could tell her,
I would let her know.

However much it pains me
To love her, I won't go.
However high she builds her walls,
Night and day, I'd love her so,

But if only I could tell her,
I would let her know.

Your Eyes, They Never Lie

Your eyes, they always tell the truth don't they?
Every smile, every tear, and every extra mile
That you take, you make, for their happiness'
sake
Your eyes, they never lie, do they never sway?

Your eyes, they never lie, they always know
what to say,
Every pain, every hurt, and when you stare at the
rain,
It falls down, to the ground, the stars can see that
now,
Your eyes, they never lie, don't they?

Your eyes can never lie, I see it when you cry
The truth is in your eyes, like a thousand
fireflies
And your tears are like the rain, ever-flowing
unlike your pain
Your eyes, you hide the stars in your eyes

Screaming Whispers of the Soul

Many words are left unspoken, unuttered, unsaid
Many people stay silent, stay frozen, stay dead,
Minds rendered catatonic, thoughts thought to be
catastrophic,
What good is a heart when the soul is an empty
shell instead?

Many countless stars litter the sky at night,
Many muses and artists, with hearts and minds
alight,
But our souls do never meet, we walk our own
empty streets,
What good is the darkness of the night without
the beauty of light?

Many countless hearts unalive, awake and
burdened,
Many broken parts arrive and take what's heard
and,
The words we speak remain unspoken, and souls
remain heartbroken,
What good is an honest word when the world
remains uncertain?

Many broken souls, with eyes that roll,
At the myriad of things that take a toll,
On encumbered spirits, and how we claim to be
restless albeit we will it,
What good is a soul without the parts that make
it whole?

What

What is a strange word to you
What is this strangest world to me
What is a stranger to do
When the stranger thing's to flee
What is the pale summer blue
What is the tint of orange haze
What is the vibrant smile in you
When I were with you and gazed
What is the silent rainy night
What is the deadening tinge of rays
What is the lambent storm of light
What is waiting for our days
What is that strangest nightly guilt
What is the stranger daily prayer
What is this home that love has built
What is wishing you were here
What is the strangest sight to behold
What is the cold and putrid graze
What is the strangest hint of gold
What is the stranger in the maze
What is that which is something to you
What is that which means nothing to me
What has absolutely nothing to do
With some breathing thing in me

In All The Wrong Places

why am i looking for love
in all the wrong places
like your heart
like this art
like this lonely, lonesome bar
why do i crave for peace
in all the wrong places
like this house
overdose
hell, nobody ever knows
why do i seek your love
in all the wrong places
like her heart
i tear myself apart
i'm torn apart

in the face of armageddon
(even if the world is ending)

even if the world is ending
i will follow you to the end
even if the stars stop burning
i will love you until the end

even if the sun is rising
far too fast and not at five
even if the moon's imploding
i'll take a leap for all of time

for in the face of armageddon
i will not fear nor will i cry
for in the face of armageddon
as long as you are here i will not die

everybody thinks i'm great
(don't patronize me)

everybody thinks i'm great
everybody thinks i'm good
everybody thinks i'm okay
i'm really, really not

everybody thinks i'm sane
everybody think's i'm cool
everybody thinks i'm nice
the sobering reality is i'm not

everybody thinks i'm honest
everybody thinks i'm funny
everybody loves me
but please leave me alone

i'm not at all that great
i'm not at all that good
i'm not at all okay
the truth is, i'm a mess

the truth is that i'm insane
the truth is that i'm uncool
the truth is that i'm quite rude
i'm not at all that nice

i know i am a liar and a fraud
i know i am unfunny and sarcastic
i know that i am abhorred
please don't ever leave

the truth is i need love
the truth is i need a hug
the truth is i can't cry
i'm a mess and i want to die

i'm not in need of pain
i don't want any sorrow
will you all still love me tomorrow
or will you leave as well

i'm a mess, a mess, a mess
so many thoughts and winding stress
so many feelings and emotions
so little time and space to move

i am in need of love
i am in need of peace
i am in need of tears
i am just a kid in fear

so please don't get confused
i'm not at all quite sane
i'm truly rotten in the brain
don't patronize me, i'm not at all that great

A Poem (Of Sorts)

poetry doesn't have to be long
nor short

it doesn't have to be confounded or confusing
nor does it have to be simple

it just has to feel
and make you feel

nature in all its splendor

the horizon of sunsets is where that big ball of
red fire in the sky meets the big blue deep waters
of the earth

and where we make art, to leave traces of our
existence for tomorrow's people to remember us
by

and where we die twice, once when we breathe
our last, and once when we're remembered
finally

our nature is to be beautiful, to try to be
remembered, but ultimately forgotten

we are the most wonderful type of dust there is

i am not alone

in a crowd i am unknown
in a group i am unseen
in the crowd i die alone
i exist but have never been

in the crowd i drown alone
i sink deep into the sea
the sea that makes me feel at home
the sea that reminds i'll never be

in the crowd i am alone
an invisible phantom ghost
in the crowd i am unknown
i am what does not matter most

i still think of suicide

i see a knife in the kitchen drawer;
and i think how many cuts it would take to kill
me.

i'm on the balcony of my building;
and i weigh whether it's the impact or the fall
that would kill me.

i don't look left and right when crossing the
street;
hoping a bus, car, or truck would run over me.

to be perfectly honest, i still think of suicide,
but i think more of all the people who love me;

An Ode to Death

o death, where is your sting
o life, what good did you bring
to this sorrow, this sorrow
when does love come in tomorrow
o death, my good and lonesome friend
o life, my beloved, when will it end
o death, my death, the friend i meet only twice
when i breathe my last, and when they say their
last goodbyes

Bipolar

in joy, i still think of death
that stinking, reeking bastard, that lies within my
breath

in sadness, i still think of life
that endless, wondering wanderer, the reason for
my strife

on love

you never really know
what it is to love someone
until you catch yourself falling
and flying all at once

you never really know
what it means to love someone
until your heart breaks
as it is being built

you never really know
until you see them whole
broken yet so whole
like a puzzle

you never really know
until their tears are visible even when they don't
cry
and until you can tell their smile
with your closed eyes

oh love is such a wondrous melody
a beautiful symphony
a magnum opus not by one
but by many

love is gazing upon another's eyes
expectant of the stars
love is hearing the rushing sea
in another's laughter

love is like floating on clouds
and sinking deep in quicksand
like the calm and the chaos all at once
and there is no peace without the panic

that's love
to have and to hold
another's heart
as if it were your own

an anthology on love and sorrow

of all the people that i know
in their hearts i seem to sow
the disparity by which we go
and how my person stooped so low

of all the people that i knew
i never thought of loving you
but all the people are not few
too many people in my view

i know i thought i saw a ghost
in this lovely haunting host
of all the people in this post
it was you i loved the most

in this place i choose to rest
in this wondrous beautiful mess
with this i puff my chest
and do what i do best

t'was a moment intertwined
when i cried with you in mind
and in this moment we remind
the love that's lost we hope we find

of the future that has passed
in the moment that is last
in the feelings of the past
we find the die that has been cast

in this endless living sea
where am i and woe is me
how did you find and see
the place where i chose to be

in you my love remains
with all the cuts and scars and stains
including all the wounds and pains
and our bruises become gains

we have not come so far
from who we really are
with you i'm not on par
for you are a burning star

and now i beg you please
if your soul i could appease
i beg again, i'm on my knees
with you i find my peace

and now i must repent
my love you are my heaven-sent
and here i now relent

time with you is time not spent

and you really are my love
a gift from the most high above
we fit the mitt like hand and glove
a beauteous bird, a godly dove

and what a love that is so clear
what a love that casts out fear
oh my darling whom i hold dear
please be close to me, please be near